Rosalind Franklin

Lara Anderson

www.heinemann.co.uk/library
Visit our website to find out more information about **Heinemann** books.

To order:
☎ Phone 44 (0) 1865 888112
📄 Send a fax to 44 (0) 1865 314091
💻 Visit the Heinemann Bookshop at **www.heinemann.co.uk/library** to browse our catalogue and order online.

Heinemann Library is an imprint of **Pearson Education Limited**, a company incorporated in England and Wales having its registered office at Edinburgh Gate, Harlow, Essex, CM20 2JE – Registered company number: 00872828

"Heinemann" is a registered trademark of Pearson Education Limited

Edited by Louise Galpine, Diyan Leake, and Adam Miller
Designed by Kimberly R. Miracle and Betsy Wernert
Original illustrations © Pearson Education Ltd
Illustrations by Mapping Specialists, Inc.
Picture research by Mica Brancic and Helen Reilly
Originated by Modern Age
Printed and bound in China by Leo Paper Group

ISBN 978 0 431044 86 6 (hardback)
13 12 11 10 09
10 9 8 7 6 5 4 3 2 1

British Library Cataloguing in Publication Data
Anderson, Lara
   Rosalind Franklin. - (Levelled biographies)
   572.8'092
A full catalogue record for this book is available from the British Library.

Acknowledgements
We would like to thank the following for permission to reproduce photographs: © AD Ltd **p. 23**; © Alamy **p. 12** (Image State); © Corbis **pp. 17** (Bettmann), **22** (Bettmann), **24** (Bettmann), **42** (Underwood & Underwood), **44** (Bettmann); © From the personal collection of Jenifer Glynn **pp. 5** (Vittorio Luzzati), **6, 7, 8, 16, 20, 21** (Vittorio Luzzati), **41, 45**; © Getty Images **pp. 9** (Fred Morley), **10** (Fred Ramage), **11** (Central Press), **39** (Time Life Pictures/Nat Farbman); © King's College, London **p. 25**; © National Medical Library/Rosalind Franklin **p. 19**; © Nature Publishing Group **p. 34**; © Newnham College Cambridge **p. 15**; © Science & Society Picture Library/Science Museum **p. 13**; © Science Photo Library **pp. 27** (Scott Camazine), **28** (A. Barrington Brown), **31, 32** (Thomas Hollyman), **37** (A. Barrington Brown), **38** (Norm Thomas), **40** (James King-Holmes), **46** (Science Source); © Shutterstock **p. 4**; © Wellcome Trust Picture Library **p. 29**.

Cover photograph of Rosalind Franklin reproduced with permission of Topfoto (© 2004 Jewish Chronicle Ltd/HIP).

We would like to thank Nancy Harris for her invaluable help in the preparation of this book.

Every effort has been made to contact copyright holders of material reproduced in this book. Any omissions will be rectified in subsequent printings if notice is given to the publishers.

Disclaimer
All the Internet addresses (URLs) given in this book were valid at the time of going to press. However, due to the dynamic nature of the Internet, some addresses may have changed, or sites may have changed or ceased to exist since publication. While the author and publishers regret any inconvenience this may cause readers, no responsibility for any such changes can be accepted by either the author or the publishers.

CONTENTS

Some words are shown in bold, **like this**. You can find out what they mean by looking in the glossary.

"Rosy" or Rosalind?

In 1968, scientist James Watson published a book called *The Double Helix*. This book told the story of one of the greatest scientific discoveries of the 20th century – the way **DNA** (deoxyribonucleic acid) is put together.

The Double Helix was a popular book, but it started a controversy that still sparks debate today. Watson wrote about a scientist he called "Rosy". He said she was secretive and argumentative. He claimed that as a woman scientist, her job should have been to assist her male colleague, Maurice Wilkins. "Rosy" was actually a real woman called Rosalind Franklin. She was a successful **physicist**. Like Watson, she had been hard at work studying DNA. But the real Rosalind could never defend herself against Watson's description of her as "Rosy". She died in 1958, before the book was published, at the age of only 37.

What is DNA?

Your body is made up of **cells**. Cells are small building blocks that make up all living things. Inside your cells are pieces of deoxyribonucleic acid (DNA). Each piece of DNA is made up of a pattern of **genes**, which are strung along pieces of DNA like beads on a string. Genes are codes that make up your physical traits, such as eye colour. A child might get blue eyes from his or her father because the code for a blue-eyed gene was passed down from father to child. For years scientists struggled to solve this puzzle. Why do we inherit physical traits like height and eye colour from our relatives? Scientists believed the answer was in the way DNA is constructed.

Franklin's beloved travels, such as this trip around Europe, were relaxing breaks from the world of science.

Franklin was a tremendous help in discovering the structure of DNA, but she never knew this. People outside the world of science might never have known of her important work if it were not for *The Double Helix*. Watson's description of "Rosy" led others to look into Franklin's role in this discovery. They found out about a woman who had dedicated her life to science. Her choice of lifestyle and career were unusual for a woman at that time. But to Franklin, science was not a choice at all—it was what she was born to do.

BIRTH OF A SCIENTIST

Rosalind Elsie Franklin was born in London on 25 July 1920, to Ellis and Muriel Franklin. Rosalind's father, Ellis, had wanted to study science as a boy, but instead he became a successful banker. Her mother, Muriel, was gentle and well educated. She preferred the roles of wife and mother rather than a career. Both Ellis and Muriel came from wealthy Jewish families who donated a lot of time and money to charity work in London. Together, they helped the Jewish community and people less fortunate than themselves. They passed on these values to their children. As a result, Rosalind grew up with a strong sense of what she felt was right and wrong.

Rosalind (second from right) poses with her siblings (from left) Roland, David, Jenifer, and Colin.

Rosalind (far right) sits on the beach with her father and brothers during a family holiday in 1926.

Rosalind enjoyed a privileged childhood. The Franklins lived in a large house at 5 Pembridge Place, which they called "5 PP". Rosalind went to private schools, spent weekends at her grandfather's mansion in the country, and travelled throughout Europe with her family.

An active mind

Maths and science appealed to Rosalind from an early age. Toys like dolls usually bored her. Instead she preferred working with her hands and challenging her mind. She spent hours working at the carpenter's workbench that her father had bought for the family.

Rosalind attended a private school in London called Norland Place. This school was unusual because boys and girls were taught in the same classes until they were 11 years old. Rosalind loved pouring her energy into athletics.

Home sweet home

When she was nine years old, Rosalind became ill with an infection. Her parents sent her to a boarding school on the coast of England called Lindores School for Young Ladies. They thought the sea air might help her to regain her strength, but she was held to a strict routine of rest and naps. She longed for home. The next year, Rosalind was finally well enough to leave Lindores.

8

Rosalind (back row, far right) enjoyed playing sports as a "Paulina".

The Paulinas

Back in London, Rosalind attended St. Paul's Girls' School, beginning in 1931. This school was a perfect match for the driven Rosalind. Many of its students, known as "Paulinas", went on to hold jobs in medicine, publishing, and law. St. Paul's also offered science courses that were just as challenging as the ones in boys' schools. Rosalind was a serious girl who worried about her studies. She released energy through team sports such as hockey and cricket, and she also played tennis. Later, she joined the school's debating team.

Rosalind delighted in all things related to science. When she was 15, she announced that she was going to be a scientist. As she worked towards her goal, she noticed that science was taught differently to girls than to boys. For boys, science was to be exciting and daring. For girls, science called for organization and repetition. This separation only fuelled her determination. Three years later, Rosalind entered Newnham College for women at the University of Cambridge.

World War II on the horizon

By the late 1930s, during Rosalind's last years at St. Paul's, Britain had begun to take notice of Adolf Hitler. Hitler was Germany's **dictator** and had a loyal following of **Nazi** Party members. They killed Jewish people and sent millions to **concentration camps**.

Kristallnacht

Thousands of Jewish homes, **synagogues**, shops, and towns throughout Germany and Austria were attacked and burned by Nazis on 9 and 10 November 1938. Smashed windows and broken glass covered the streets. The night is now known as "Kristallnacht", which means "Crystal Night". Thousands of men were taken to concentration camps. Wives and children were left without homes. In response, Britain welcomed **refugee** children who were up to 17 years old. Some went to foster families or orphanages and some worked on farms. The Franklins fostered two Austrian girls. One of these girls, Evi Eisenstadter, was 9 years old. Ellis Franklin spoke to her in German, and she called him Father Franklin. She kept in touch with the Franklins for years afterwards.

Approximately 10,000 children arrived safely from Germany before Britain entered World War II on 1 September 1939.

Working women

Before World War II (1939–1945), almost five million women in Britain had jobs outside the home. Young, unmarried women enjoyed this new feeling of earning their own money. Married women or women who came from wealthy families did not need to work. The better off women devoted their spare time to charities.

This photograph shows one of the "balloon girls" handling a barrage balloon (with one in the background). These balloons were used as weapons against enemy aircraft. They were a common sight in London by 1939.

When the war started, British men joined the armed forces or participated in the war effort in other ways. More women were needed to take over jobs previously done by men. Women could earn as much as 40 shillings (£2) per week. This was a reasonable wage in the 1940s, but it was less than men were paid for doing the same jobs. Women worked on farms, in offices, and in factories, producing goods needed for the war effort. They worked on bridges, railways, buses, and helped to build aeroplanes. A team of women built Waterloo Bridge in London in 1937. It is still sometimes called the Ladies Bridge.

The Franklins were a wealthy family, so Rosalind did not need to work. Both she and her mother helped with charities and refugee committees. "Paulinas" were released early every day to help with filing and other office work at the refugee committee headquarters in London.

Make do and mend

Clothing rations during World War II changed the way women dressed. Materials such as wool were used to make uniforms for soldiers, so the amount of fabric available to women was limited. They were encouraged to "make do and mend". They turned old blankets into skirts and coats, and turned pillowcases into shorts and tops.

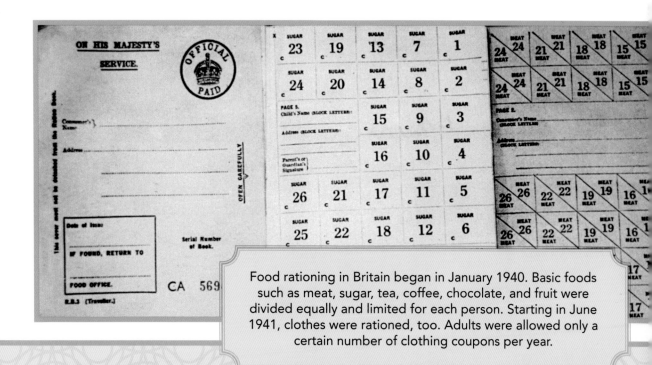

Food rationing in Britain began in January 1940. Basic foods such as meat, sugar, tea, coffee, chocolate, and fruit were divided equally and limited for each person. Starting in June 1941, clothes were rationed, too. Adults were allowed only a certain number of clothing coupons per year.

SCIENCE AND WAR

College life at Cambridge

Franklin entered Newnham, a women's college at the University of Cambridge, in 1938. She was 18 years old. Cambridge offered the best scientific education in Britain. But its rules were unfair to women. Until the 1930s, female students had to sit together in the front rows of men's lectures. Even women of importance, such as the Newnham principal, did not participate in important events. Instead they were required to sit with the wives of male teachers. It was not until 1939 that Cambridge employed Dorothy Garrod, the school's first female professor.

Students in Cambridge still enjoy boating on the River Cam.

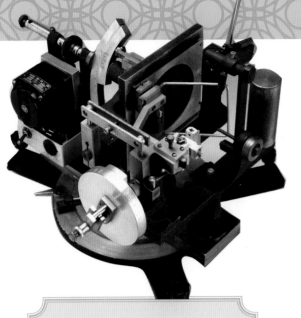

Franklin probably used an
X-ray diffraction camera similar
to this one from 1940.

What is crystallography?

Some biological molecules, such as **DNA**, can form crystals. They are so tiny that scientists use X-rays to see inside them. When an X-ray beam is passed through a crystal, a pattern appears on a photographic plate. These patterns provide important clues about the structure of the crystal. Crystallography is also sometimes called **X-ray diffraction**. Franklin would later use this technique to study DNA.

Despite these restrictions, Franklin enjoyed university. Her parents provided her with a generous allowance, but her letters home bragged of bargain hunting, as she bought secondhand items and textbooks. She took difficult classes and liked to attend lectures and meetings. Professor William Bragg spoke at one of these meetings. He was a great scientist, known as the "father of **crystallography**". This is a method of using X-rays to see inside **molecules**, tiny particles made up of groups of **atoms**. His work fascinated Franklin. In the future she would use crystallography in some of her most important work.

Franklin worked long hours in the science **laboratory**. In her spare time she enjoyed sports like hockey and tennis. She liked to ride her bicycle and go boating on the River Cam. Once Franklin rode her bike from Cambridge to London. Her parents were not pleased. "Why are you so surprised about cycling home?" she asked in a letter. "I want my bike in London, and it seems the simplest way of getting there. . . . It isn't very far." Cambridge to London is in fact about 80 kilometres (50 miles).

Wartime living

World War II officially broke out in 1939, during Franklin's second year at Cambridge. Many science teachers left to help in the war effort. As a result, students had to be more independent in their studies and work. Franklin was very much an independent student, so this did not stop her from continuing in her quest to become a scientist.

Air-raid warnings

"We do not so far have to carry gas masks," Franklin wrote to her parents, "but apparently we do have to spend hours in trenches every time there is a warning." Britain was at risk of being attacked by bombs. Air-raid drills at Cambridge signalled that everyone should move to protective trenches dug nearby. Franklin was responsible for waking ten people during these warnings.

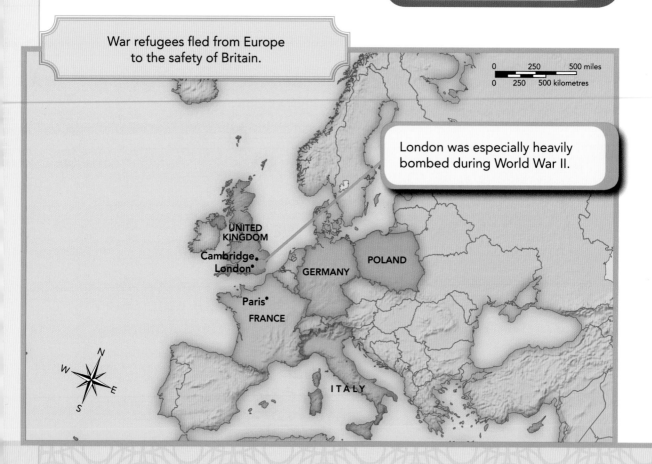

War refugees fled from Europe to the safety of Britain.

London was especially heavily bombed during World War II.

0   250   500 miles

0   250   500 kilometres

UNITED KINGDOM

Cambridge
London

GERMANY

POLAND

Paris

FRANCE

ITALY

N W E S

Activist and chef

Many people in Europe lost their homes during the war. Some were allowed to move to the safety of the United States and Britain. But only a very limited number were allowed to move. Franklin thought this limitation was unfair. She joined a group in Cambridge that raised money for **refugee** aid so that more people could enter Britain safely. She also volunteered during the university holidays to help Jewish war refugees from Europe.

Normal college activities such as parties, picnics, and dances were rare during wartime, but Franklin still found ways to enjoy herself. She also studied hard and worked long hours in the science laboratory. She sometimes took holidays and began cooking for friends. Good ingredients were hard to find during the war, but she experimented with what was available. She once walked into a shop and saw a basket of eggs. She was overjoyed when the shopkeeper told her to take four. That night, she remembered, "We had real fried eggs with bits of fried bread for Sunday supper, a feast which is still quite a great pleasure to look back on."

Newnham is one of 31 colleges that make up the University of Cambridge. Cambridge's reputation has not changed since Franklin was a student. It is considered one of the best universities in the world.

Friends in science

Franklin met Adrienne Weill, a Jewish French scientist, during her third year at Cambridge. The two women got along straight away. In 1941, Franklin moved into the house that Weill rented out to students. She delighted in the busy mixture of English and French discussions going on at any time. She improved her French accent. She also learned to argue and debate in a good-natured, intelligent way. Franklin was not a **feminist**, but she did want to be considered as seriously devoted to her work as any male scientist. She found Weill, who had studied with Marie Curie (see box), to be a great source of knowledge and comfort.

Adrienne Weill was Franklin's close friend and fellow student.

Perfectionist

Franklin worked and studied so hard during her last term at Newnham that she was exhausted as her final exams approached. Her marks suffered because of this. She earned the second highest mark possible, but Franklin had hoped for the absolute highest. Still, she was awarded a research **scholarship** under Professor R. G. W. Norrish. Franklin and Norrish did not get along. She turned to Weill for advice. Eventually, Franklin decided to leave Norrish's laboratory. She wanted to concentrate on something connected more closely to the war effort.

Marie Curie

Marie Curie was a noted pioneer in the field of **radioactivity**. This is when **elements** give off rays of energy. Elements are substances that cannot be separated into simpler substances. Iron and carbon are two examples of elements. Curie was the first woman to be awarded two **Nobel Prizes**, in 1903 and 1911. She is the only person to win a Nobel Prize in two different science fields: **physics** and chemistry. Curie's work and success paved the way for women scientists of Franklin's time, but attitudes towards women were slow to change.

INDEPENDENT WOMAN

Many young female scientists found jobs as teachers during World War II. They were replacing men who had left to do war-related research. Franklin did not want to teach. She wanted to help in the war effort. In 1942, just after her 22nd birthday, she became the assistant research officer at the British Coal Utilization Research Association. It was known as BCURA.

The holes in coal

BCURA was an industrial organization that researched the use of coal. When Franklin arrived, the staff was full of young people. BCURA had been bombed early in the war, and many of its buildings had been destroyed. The scientists who worked there had to move to other work spaces around London. Franklin enjoyed this independence, and she was delighted to be working with coal. It was used for railways, heating houses, powering factories, and testing gas masks during World War II.

Coal is made of carbon. At BCURA, Franklin identified two classes of carbons: **graphitizing** and **non-graphitizing** carbon. She accomplished this by experimenting with coal. Her work included heating, measuring, and examining the carbon content of different types of coal.

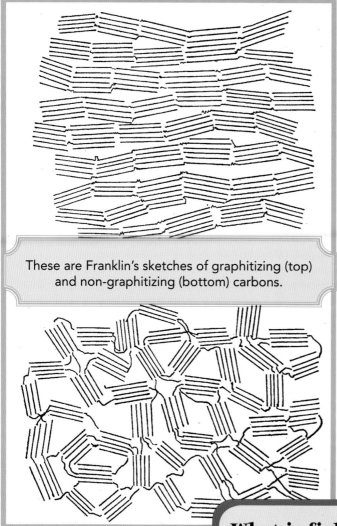

These are Franklin's sketches of graphitizing (top) and non-graphitizing (bottom) carbons.

Independence allowed Franklin to work happily and tirelessly. In her four years at BCURA, she contributed to two scientific papers and wrote three on her own. These papers, published in scientific **journals**, represented her experimental **data** (information). Scientists sometimes still use these papers today. These were great accomplishments, and Franklin was happy at BCURA. She sewed brightly coloured patches on her lab coats to spice them up, and she became confident in her work.

The war ended in 1945. Franklin was ready for a change. She was hoping to find something with more fieldwork (see box) than was available to her at BCURA.

What is fieldwork?

When scientists do hands-on research to collect new information, it is called fieldwork. Typically, it is done "in situ", which means "in the place". This allows scientists to examine a subject in exactly the place it occurs. Franklin did fieldwork when studying **DNA**.

A love for Paris

In 1946, Franklin guided two French scientists, Jacques Mering and Marcel Mathieu, around the sights of London. Mathieu was a close friend of Adrienne Weill. Weill talked to Mathieu about hiring Franklin to work in his Paris **laboratory**, and he offered Franklin a job. She moved to Paris in February 1947, when she was 26 years old.

The Central State Chemistry Laboratories in Paris, where Franklin worked, were known as the "labo" to staff. She liked her colleagues and formed a close bond with Mering. It has been said that all the women at the "labo," including Franklin, were just a little in love with him.

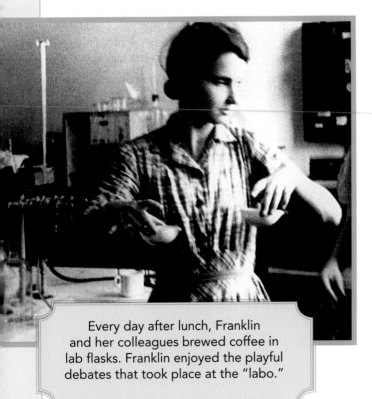

Every day after lunch, Franklin and her colleagues brewed coffee in lab flasks. Franklin enjoyed the playful debates that took place at the "labo."

Friends in France

At the "labo" in Paris, Franklin could speak freely with colleagues. Everyone engaged happily in discussions about science, politics, and work. Eventually, she was able to speak French fluently. Franklin and her colleagues ate their lunch together every day. Outside work, they went on picnics and camping trips together. They would swim at a nearby pool and go out dancing at night.

Mering taught Franklin the techniques of **X-ray diffraction**, or **crystallography**. She would later use this method in her DNA experiments. But she never considered herself a crystallographer. Rather, she was someone who used its methods.

Franklin fell in love with France. She missed it long after she left. But she knew her move to Paris was temporary. In 1950, after four years in Paris, Franklin decided to move back to London.

"I've been told my French is best when I'm angry.... I had a glorious row this a.m.... I enjoyed it immensely.... It's odd but I couldn't do it in English with a straight face. Here a battle of words is a sort of game which nobody takes seriously."

Franklin wrote this in a letter to her parents.

Franklin's good friend and colleague at the "labo", Vittorio Luzzati, took this snapshot in France.

DÉFENSE ABSOLUE
de FUMER
DANS LES DORTOIRS

Secrets of DNA

Methods of **crystallography** had improved by the late 1940s. Scientists could study tiny **molecules** from living things. After World War II, the hottest topic in science was the secret of the **gene**. In 1951, Franklin joined Professor John Randall's staff at King's College **laboratory** in London.

Resourceful Rosalind

Scientists in London were beginning to use **X-ray diffraction** to study biological subjects. When Franklin arrived at King's College, the staff was borrowing an X-ray machine from a military department. Franklin's first task was to order equipment for the staff's own X-ray machine. She also designed an X-ray camera to be made by King's College's workshops.

Randall was hopeful that crystallography would lead to more knowledge about genes. Exactly how **genetic** information was stored and transferred was a mystery in 1951. Scientists were grappling with the question of how **DNA** is put together and how it works.

What did scientists know about DNA at the time?

In 1865, an Austrian scientist named Gregor Mendel (right) discovered that genes pass on physical traits. He used pea plants to conduct his experiments. Mendel tracked the physical traits parent peas passed down to the new plants (offspring) they produced. By 1905, scientists knew that genes in living **cells** are strung together like beads on a string.

In 1911, the scientist Thomas Morgan studied fruit flies in his "fly lab" in New York. There he made an important observation called "cross fertilization", or "crossing over". This showed him how **chromosomes** worked. Chromosomes are long pieces of DNA inside **cells**. In "cross fertilization", one chromosome actually exchanges information with, or crosses over to, another chromosome. Morgan, like other scientists, was not sure if the DNA or the protein of a cell caused this exchange. In 1952, the scientists Martha Chase and Alfred Hershey proved that it was in fact the DNA and not the protein.

But the question remained: how does the genetic information (the gene) get from the old chromosome to the new one? Scientists needed more information. King's College set about solving the problem.

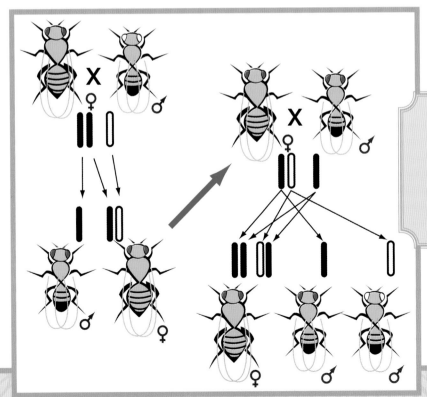

This diagram shows the findings of Morgan's fruit fly experiments. In this example, the information for the flies' eye colour is being crossed over.

Separation at King's College

After four happy years in Paris, Franklin found London to be depressing. Food was still rationed and **makeshift housing** was everywhere, sheltering the people whose homes had been bombed during the war. King's College was not the lively work environment she had enjoyed in Paris. Women were not allowed to lunch with their male colleagues, and Franklin found it difficult to get to know her peers.

Clashing personalities

Franklin found it especially hard to befriend her colleague Maurice Wilkins, a scientist from New Zealand. Wilkins had started working on the DNA puzzle before Franklin came to King's. He was excited to learn that she would be joining the King's staff, but he was away on holiday when Franklin arrived.

Maurice Wilkins later shared the 1962 **Nobel Prize** with James Watson and Francis Crick.

Professor Randall gave some of the DNA work to Franklin without discussing it with Wilkins. Franklin thought Randall wanted her to work independently, but Wilkins thought they were to work as part of the same team. Wilkins did not learn until years later that Randall had assigned part of the DNA work to Franklin while he was away. So, while Franklin was simply carrying on with her research, Wilkins thought she was trying to take over his DNA work. They both thought the other one was impossible to talk to. Franklin was vocal and enjoyed a good argument. Wilkins was quiet and backed away from confrontation. They never got on while Franklin was at King's.

One of Franklin's only friends at King's College was Raymond Gosling, a **graduate student**. He had been doing research on DNA and was assigned to work with Franklin.

"If you believed what you were saying, you had to argue strongly with Rosalind if she thought you were wrong, whereas Maurice would simply shut up…. [Rosalind] always expected me to justify myself very strongly…. And of course I found this a tremendous help. I learned a lot from her that way."

Raymond Gosling discusses what it was like to work with Franklin and Wilkins.

A new discovery

Franklin and Gosling worked well together. They took fantastic X-ray diffraction photographs of DNA. In 1951 Franklin discovered something no one else had before—two forms of DNA. She named them "A" and "B". These were important clues in determining the structure of DNA. Franklin wanted to share her findings with other scientists.

Scientific sharing

Scientists like to meet with other scientists to get opinions on ideas and experiments. They can then decide if it is worth taking a closer look at a project or discovery. Scientists do not like to waste time researching or experimenting on leads that turn out to be meaningless. They usually do not give away all of their information at these meetings. Details of their work are published in scientific **journals**.

Scientists keep track of their progress by writing details about their work. In this way, science can keep a history and record itself over time. As a result, most major discoveries are traceable through scientific journals. It is fairly easy to determine who contributed what, even with a problem that might have taken years to solve.

Meanwhile, Franklin and Wilkins were still struggling to get along. Randall decided that Franklin would concentrate on the "A" form while Wilkins would handle the "B" form. From then on, Franklin and Wilkins stopped communicating almost completely.

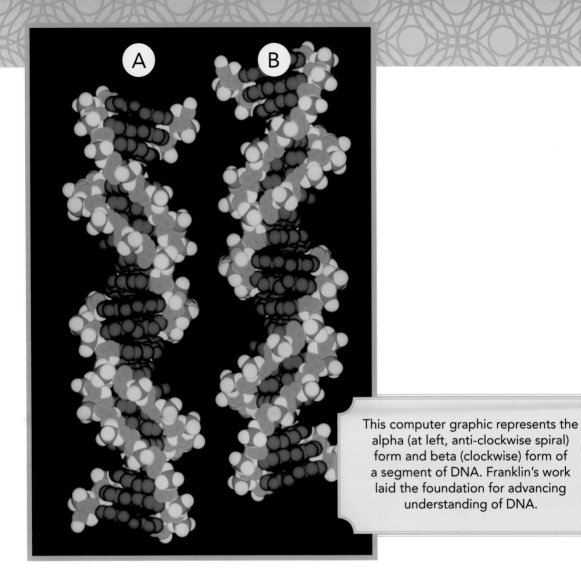

This computer graphic represents the alpha (at left, anti-clockwise spiral) form and beta (clockwise) form of a segment of DNA. Franklin's work laid the foundation for advancing understanding of DNA.

Wilkins felt lonely at King's. He began to visit fellow scientists James Watson and Francis Crick at the Cavendish laboratory at the University of Cambridge.

In 1951, Franklin gave a talk at King's College. James Watson was in the audience, but he did not pay attention when Franklin spoke about the "A" and "B" forms of DNA. Even though Franklin's observations would turn out to be huge clues in solving the mystery of DNA's structure, no one at the meeting really felt that a major discovery was on the horizon.

The first DNA model

After Franklin's talk at King's, Watson went back to the Cavendish laboratory at Cambridge and told his research partner, Crick, everything he remembered. Just like Watson, Crick was extremely interested in DNA. Together, they decided to build a model of DNA. Unfortunately, Watson had not taken notes when Franklin spoke. He missed a major clue.

Francis Crick (shown here) became great friends with Franklin a few years later, after she left King's College.

Watson and Crick invited the staff from King's lab to see their completed model. Franklin knew instantly that it was wrong. She immediately pointed out the problem—where was the water? Franklin knew that DNA is a thirsty molecule. It needed ten times the amount of water they had included. The model would not hold together the way they had built it. After this major mistake, the directors of both laboratories decided that the staff at King's would handle all research.

However, this did not hurt the friendship formed between Watson, Crick, and Wilkins. Still feeling left out at King's, Wilkins discussed his DNA work with Watson and Crick. He also talked about his problems with Franklin. Meanwhile, Franklin was still studying the "A" form of DNA. She concluded that its shape was not a **helix**, or spiral shape. (This would be proved wrong later.) Franklin playfully wrote a death notice and gave a mock funeral for the double helix in the "A" form.

IT IS WITH GREAT REGRET THAT WE HAVE TO ANNOUNCE THE DEATH, ON FRIDAY 18TH JULY 1952 OF D.N.A. HELIX (CRYSTALLINE)

DEATH FOLLOWED A PROTRACTED ILLNESS WHICH AN INTENSIVE COURSE OF BESSELISED INJECTIONS HAD FAILED TO RELIEVE.

A MEMORIAL SERVICE WILL BE HELD NEXT MONDAY OR TUESDAY.

IT IS HOPED THAT DR. M.H.F. WILKINS WILL SPEAK IN MEMORY OF THE LATE HELIX

R. E. Franklin   R. G. Gosling

It is important to note that this silly document has come to symbolize Franklin's belief that DNA was not a double helix at all. This is not true. She always believed the "B" form was a helix, but had trouble proving that the "A" form was as well.

AN UNDECLARED RACE

Restless at King's

As 1952 began, Franklin's thoughts were beginning to lead her away from King's College. She was lonely, and her difficult relationship with Wilkins did not help. She visited scientist John Desmond Bernal at Birkbeck College in London to talk about the possibility of working in his **laboratory**. Bernal liked the idea of Franklin joining his staff, but there were no openings at the time. This did not bother Franklin. She was moving along with her **DNA** research and was happy with the work she was doing. In the spring she was able to take a break. She joined a friend on a walking tour of North Wales.

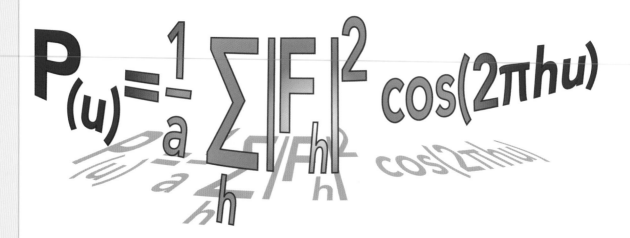

Franklin used the complex Patterson Function, shown here, to decode the mathematical meaning in her photographs.

This image shows "Photograph 51". Bernal once said, "As a scientist Miss Franklin was distinguished by extreme clarity and perfection in everything she undertook. Her photographs are among the most beautiful X-ray photographs of any substance ever taken."

Photograph 51

In May, Franklin developed an image of the "B" form of DNA that showed a remarkably clear "X" pattern of stripes in the centre. It was the clearest picture of the "B" form ever produced. It was unquestionably a double **helix**. Usually Franklin used a technique called the Patterson Function to determine the mathematical meaning of an image. It took long hours of calculations and concentration. (Luckily, it can now be done in seconds by a computer.) Randall had decided earlier that Franklin was to concentrate only on the "A" form of DNA. So, she immediately set this new photograph of the "B" form aside without spending much time on it. This photograph is now famously referred to by the number Franklin assigned to it—"Photograph 51".

Linus Pauling is the only person to receive two **Nobel Prizes** that were not shared with another person. In 1954 he was awarded a Nobel Prize for chemistry, and in 1962 he was awarded a Nobel Peace Prize.

Let the race begin

In 1953, U.S. scientist Linus Pauling thought he had cracked the DNA problem. He built a model and wrote a paper on his findings. He sent a copy of the paper to his son, Peter, who was studying at Cambridge. Peter showed Pauling's paper to Watson and Crick. Watson immediately saw that Pauling's model was similar to the incorrect model he and Crick built earlier. They were delighted. They could still be the first scientists to figure out the structure of DNA. But Pauling would soon realize his mistake. Watson and Crick thought they had to work fast if they wanted to beat him to the finish line. Interestingly, they were the only two who looked at solving the structure of DNA as a race. Pauling, Franklin, and Wilkins were all unaware that a race existed at all.

While Watson and Crick attacked the DNA puzzle yet again, Franklin was busy preparing to leave King's College. Bernal had finally offered her a job in his laboratory at Birkbeck, and she accepted.

A surprising visit

After Pauling published his incorrect model, Watson visited the King's laboratory. He wanted to show Franklin Pauling's mistake, since she had been quick to point out a similar mistake that he and Crick had made with their earlier model. In his book *The Double Helix*, Watson says he knocked on Franklin's door and could tell instantly that he was unwelcome. However, Franklin later told a friend that one day she came back into her room to find someone reading her notebooks. She did not say if this person was Watson.

James Watson gives his version of events in *The Double Helix*.

"Suddenly Rosy came from behind the lab bench that separated us and began moving towards me. Fearing that in her hot anger she might strike me, I grabbed up the Pauling manuscript and hastily retreated to the open door."

And the winner is...

Wilkins was busy doing his own DNA work, and he liked to get together with Watson and Crick to discuss his findings. Unaware that Watson and Crick were determined more than ever to work out the structure of DNA, Wilkins talked openly. He shared some critical information.

Wilkins was extremely frustrated with Franklin on a day when Watson visited King's. Wilkins showed Watson some of Franklin's work, including "Photograph 51". That night, Wilkins and Watson went to dinner. Watson pressed Wilkins for the mathematical meaning of the pattern on the photograph. Wilkins gave it to him. On the train back to Cambridge, Watson sketched a pattern from memory in the margin of a newspaper.

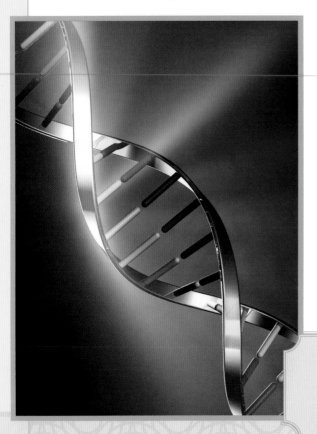

Watson and Crick had another piece of critical information—Franklin's unpublished report on her latest DNA **data**. This report was not marked as confidential, so it was assumed that anyone could read it. They had everything they needed to build their model. But how did the chemicals in DNA actually fit together? Watson worked tirelessly until he worked it out. In March 1953, he and Crick built the correct DNA model.

Watson and Crick proved that DNA is in the shape of a double helix, shown here. A double helix is like two phone cords spiralling around each other.

James Watson discusses the moment he understood the mystery of DNA.

"The instant I saw the picture my mouth fell open and my pulse began to race."

17th March draft

In the spring of 1953, Franklin wrote a paper for the scientific **journal** *Nature*. The paper was dated 17 March, 1953, one day before she learned of Watson and Crick's DNA model. Franklin's paper summarized her findings on DNA up to that point. She had everything correct. She needed only to work out how the chemicals in DNA actually fit together. When she received news of the Watson and Crick model, she only slightly changed her paper. Then she submitted it to *Nature*. Her paper was published alongside Watson and Crick's DNA findings on 25 April, 1953. Franklin's paper was viewed as supporting evidence rather than as her own independent discoveries.

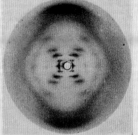

Sodium deoxyribose nucleate from calf thymus, Structure B

What Franklin never knew

Franklin and Wilkins were supportive of Watson and Crick's discovery. Scientists are generally happy to see a problem solved. Franklin knew the model was correct as soon as she saw it. This is not surprising, since the model was based largely on her work. Watson and Crick never told Franklin just how much of her information they used, and Franklin never found out. Watson and Crick could have offered to publish their findings with hers. They could have admitted to using her photograph and data. They could have thanked Franklin and Wilkins for providing these vital clues. But they did not.

So close

With the DNA problem solved, Franklin felt the time was right to leave King's. She was excited to be going to Birkbeck College. Randall told her to leave her DNA work at King's. This did not bother her, even though she knew that Wilkins planned to repeat her research after she left. But Randall ordered her not to contact or communicate with anyone from King's after she was gone. But Franklin had been Gosling's **supervisor** and friend at King's. She could not abandon him. The two met secretly, and Franklin helped him finish his **Ph.D**. They even published a few papers together on DNA.

Years later, Franklin's friend, a writer named Anne Sayre, interviewed Crick. She asked him if anyone at King's would have worked out the structure of DNA. He replied, "Oh, don't be silly. Of course, Rosalind would have solved it. . . . With Rosalind it was only a matter of time." But Franklin had already decided to leave King's. She probably did not realize how close she was to the solution.

"I do not remember her feeling that she had lost a competition, only that something exciting had been discovered."

Franklin's sister, Jenifer Glynn, discusses her sister in 1996.

James Watson (left) and Francis Crick standing next to their DNA model.

LIFE AFTER DNA

A new beginning

Franklin began work at Birkbeck College in March 1953. She was excited to work for J. D. Bernal. He was a scientist she admired, and Birkbeck was certainly an improvement over the atmosphere at King's. Bernal was known for his equal treatment of men and women. Franklin liked this about him. Bernal encouraged women to get ahead in their careers, and he looked for opportunities for them. Franklin felt respected and supported at Birkbeck.

Bernal was an Irish-born scientist. He is known mainly for being one of the earliest scientists to work with X-ray **crystallography**. He earned the nickname Sage, which means "wise", because of his brilliant mind.

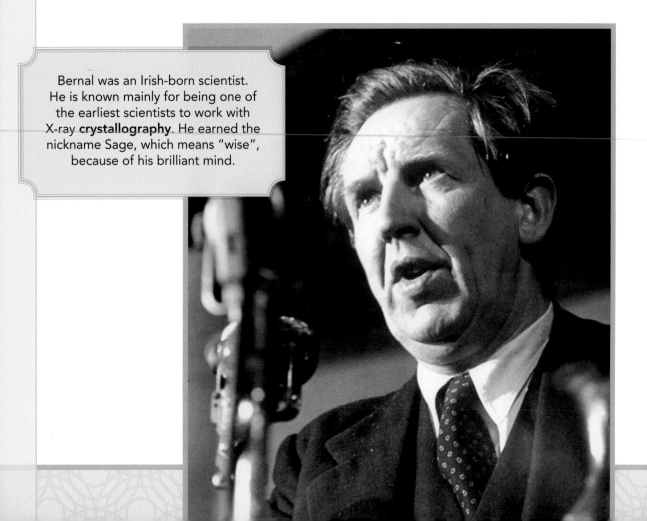

The problem with viruses

Bernal wanted Franklin to immediately start on X-ray work on the TMV **virus** (a living thing that causes disease). TMV, or Tobacco Mosaic Virus, is a plant virus that Bernal had been studying for years. He wanted Franklin to pick up where he had left off and discover the structure of the virus. Once this was determined, scientists would know more about all plant viruses and even some animal viruses. This was important because a lot of these viruses affected the crops of farmers. TMV does not just infect tobacco. It infects at least 125 individual plants, including tomatoes, peppers, cucumbers, and even flowers. It is a difficult virus to control. Bernal thought that if anyone could do it, Franklin could.

TMV causes tobacco leaves to curl and discolour in patches. It is highly infectious and easily spread. Learning the structure of the virus was the first step in working out how it caused disease. Franklin's job was to find out where the virus's **genetic** material, **RNA**, was located.

The beginning of a friendship

A South African scientist called Aaron Klug joined Birkbeck shortly after Franklin. He liked to argue and debate just like Franklin. They became great friends. It was the longest and happiest relationship she ever had with a colleague.

"She noticed everything. The fact that she produced the best specimens of TMV wasn't due to chance.... It's an art, doing this, it's a matter of the pains she took... the keeping track of things, the noticing. That's how discoveries are made. And this was one of Rosalind's greatest gifts."

Aaron Klug discusses his friend.

Klug was awarded the **Nobel Prize** in chemistry in 1982.

A tough time

Franklin worked in gloomy conditions. Her **laboratory** was on the fifth floor of an old house that had been bombed during the war. Her X-ray equipment was down in the cellar. There was no lift, so she had to climb the stairs many times a day. The roof in her room leaked. She placed beakers and pots around to catch the drips. Franklin did not complain. She was happy with her work and content with what she was given.

In 1955, the Agricultural Research Council, which had been supporting her work, stopped funding her experiments. Franklin was hurt. Klug said this was the only time he ever saw her in tears. Franklin strongly believed that her funding was denied because "the ARC refuses to support any project that has a woman directing it." She even applied to the U.S. Public Health Service for funding. She had received some positive feedback from the United States before the ARC finally granted funding for three more years.

Franklin, seen here mountain climbing in Norway, was an expert at finding cheap travel deals. She liked travelling with hardly any money because "then you needed your wits".

Franklin was enjoying this chapter of her life. She had her own comfortable flat. She went to parties and visited friends. She earned a modest income, but she preferred saving over spending. Even on her beloved travels, she always found ways to save money.

A LIFE CUT SHORT

Summer in the United States

Franklin spent the summer of 1956 visiting friends and science **laboratories** in the United States. Her American friend Anne Sayre was in London that summer. Franklin insisted that Sayre stay in her flat while she was gone. When Sayre arrived, she was shocked to find "how very noticing Rosalind was, for everything in the refrigerator or on the shelves catered precisely to my likings . . . nothing missing, nothing wrongly chosen. . . . She had a thoughtfulness which I admired."

Becoming ill

Franklin enjoyed her time in the United States, but she began having stomach pains. When she returned to London, she learned that she needed an operation. Franklin had cancer of the ovaries, which are part of the female reproductive system. Shortly after her first operation, she learned that she needed a second one. Franklin did not want her family to worry and fuss over her as she recovered. She had become good friends with Francis Crick after she left King's, so she stayed with Crick and his wife. Franklin viewed these operations as minor interruptions to her work. The second operation was successful, and no more cancer was found. She claimed she was cured.

The will to work

In January 1957, Franklin was strong enough to go back to Birkbeck. She never told anyone there of her illness. She secretly slipped away from the laboratory to undergo cancer therapy. In the last few months of her life, Franklin became interested in the polio **virus**. Everyone warned her to be careful. It is a dangerous virus that can be deadly. By then, she knew the cancer was going to prevent her from living a full life. The threat of polio did not scare her. She even stored the virus in a thermos flask in her parents' refrigerator at one point! Her mother was not happy about this.

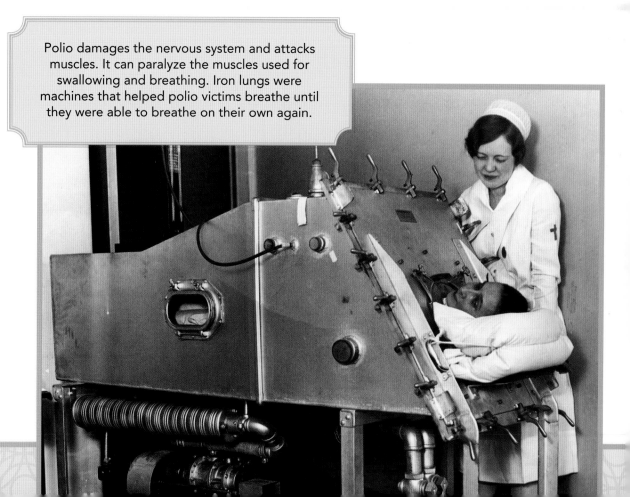

Polio damages the nervous system and attacks muscles. It can paralyze the muscles used for swallowing and breathing. Iron lungs were machines that helped polio victims breathe until they were able to breathe on their own again.

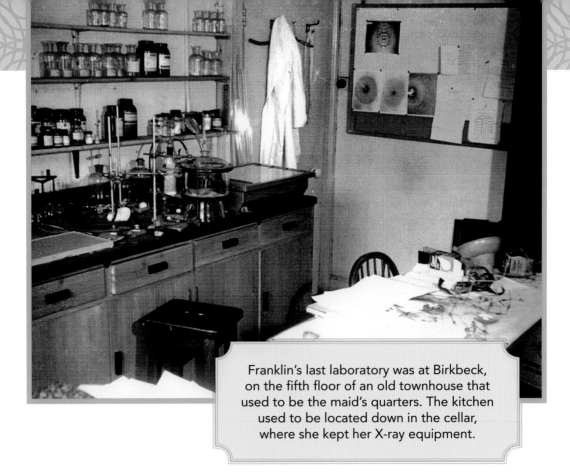

Franklin's last laboratory was at Birkbeck, on the fifth floor of an old townhouse that used to be the maid's quarters. The kitchen used to be located down in the cellar, where she kept her X-ray equipment.

Gone too soon

Franklin's work still thrived. She received a request to build TMV models for the virus exhibition at the Brussels World Fair in Belgium. She was planning trips to attend conferences in the United States and Vienna in 1958.

Franklin worked as much as possible and tried to live as normally as possible. She went to restaurants, visited friends, and went on holiday in Switzerland. She even planned a big party for her parents' 40th wedding anniversary. She remained optimistic and full of hope. She was not depressed. If anything, the anger she had felt towards illness as a child now resurfaced against her disease as an adult. She fought hard to get better, but she only got worse. This was one great fight she would not win. Rosalind Franklin died on 16 April, 1958. She was only 37 years old.

The question remains

In 1962, James Watson, Francis Crick, and Maurice Wilkins were awarded **Nobel Prizes**. The prizes were for their work in physiology, or medicine, for their parts in discovering **DNA's** double-**helix** structure. As a rule, the Nobel Prize can only be awarded to living persons and to no more than three people at once. Franklin was not a contender for the award because she was no longer living. The question remains whether or not she would have been considered if she were alive to receive it. History has shown that if Watson and Crick had not had Franklin's data and "Photograph 51", they could not have worked out the correct model for DNA when they did. Without this information, it is likely that Linus Pauling or Franklin herself would have beaten them to it.

Nobel Prize winners Wilkins (far left), Crick (third from left), and Watson (second from right) pose for photographers.

ROSALIND, NOT "ROSY"

It has been suggested that Watson created the character "Rosy" in his book *The Double **Helix*** to downplay her important work and emphasize his own. Franklin's family, friends, and fellow scientists, including Crick, agree that "Rosy" was more Watson's invention than she was a real person.

Francis Crick tells author Anne Sayre about how the character of "Rosy" came to exist.

"What Jim [Watson] put down in his book is all ideas he had from Maurice [Wilkins]. Jim never really knew Rosalind. . . . And Maurice had very fixed ideas which Jim accepted. I told him they were wrong."

Rosalind Franklin will be remembered in history as exactly the person she set out to be—a scientist.

Franklin never knew how much of her work was used in the understanding of DNA, nor that she was not properly credited. Watson was not the only one to leave Franklin out of history. Linus Pauling wrote that Wilkins discovered the "B" form of **DNA**. We now know that it was Franklin, not Wilkins, who produced those remarkable photographs, including the most famous, "Photograph 51".

Remembering Rosalind

Eventually, people began to listen, ask questions, and take action so that Rosalind Franklin would not be forgotten. Friends and colleagues published books and articles that have helped to bring the real Rosalind to life. They have proved that her work was critical to Watson and Crick's remarkable achievement. Awards and **scholarships** have been named in her honour. King's College has named an educational building after Franklin and Wilkins, Birkbeck College has a Rosalind Franklin **laboratory**, and Newnham College has built a house for students called the Rosalind Franklin Building. In 2004, the Chicago Medical School changed its name to the Rosalind Franklin University of Medicine and Science. Finally, 50 years after Franklin's untimely death, her enormous contributions to the world of science are being recognized. Rosalind Franklin will always be remembered as a woman whose dedication and drive opened new pathways for future scientists.

TIMELINES

Franklin's life

1920	Rosalind Elsie Franklin is born in London.
1932	Franklin enters St. Paul's Girls' School.
1938	Franklin enters Newnham College at the University of Cambridge.
1941	Franklin earns her degree and a research **scholarship** to work with the scientist R. G. W. Norrish.
1942	Franklin begins work at BCURA.
1947	Franklin moves to Paris to work in Jacques Mering's **laboratory**.
1951	Franklin moves back to London and begins working at King's College.
1952	Franklin produces "Photograph 51".
DECEMBER 1952	James Watson and Francis Crick gain access to Franklin's unpublished report, which details her findings on the structure of **DNA**.
JANUARY 1953	Linus Pauling publishes an incorrect proposal for a DNA model.
FEBRUARY 1953	Watson and Crick build the correct DNA model.

MARCH 1953	Franklin's DNA findings are written in a paper dated 17 March. News of James Watson and Francis Crick's model reaches her. Franklin begins work at Birkbeck College.
25 APRIL 1953	Watson and Crick's paper with the correct proposal for DNA is published in the scientific **journal** *Nature*.
1954	Aaron Klug joins the staff at Birkbeck.
1956	Franklin visits the United States. She learns she has cancer of the ovaries on her return to Britain.
1957	Franklin researches the polio **virus** at Birkbeck.
16 APRIL 1958	Franklin dies.

World timeline

1857 Gregor Mendel conducts his pea experiment.

1869 Johann Friedrich Miescher finds a substance in human white blood **cells**. This will later be known as **DNA**.

1903 Marie Curie is awarded the **Nobel Prize** in **physics** along with her husband, Pierre Curie, and physicist Henri Becquerel for their discovery of **radioactivity**.

1911 Marie Curie is awarded the Nobel Prize in chemistry for her work in radioactivity.

1912 The *Titanic* sinks in the North Atlantic after hitting an iceberg.

1914 World War I begins.

1918 World War I ends. In Britain, women householders (people who own or rent the home in which they live) over the age of 30 are given voting rights.

1921 Albert Einstein wins the Nobel Prize.

1924 The first Winter Olympics are held.

1928 All women in Britain over the age of 21 are given voting rights.

1929 The stock market crashes and the Great Depression begins.

1931 The tallest building in the world at the time, the Empire State Building, is completed in New York City.

1933 Adolf Hitler's **Nazi** Party wins power in Germany.

NOVEMBER 1938 Jewish homes and businesses are attacked by the Nazis on "Kristallnacht".

1939	Germany invades Poland. France and Britain declare war on Germany and World War II begins.
1940	Thomas Morgan starts his "fly lab".
DECEMBER **1941**	Japan attacks Pearl Harbor and the United States enters World War II.
1942	The Holocaust (murdering of Jewish civilians in Europe during World War II) begins.
1944	Oswald Avery discovers that DNA is responsible for **genetic** material. Most scientists still believed that DNA was too simple to be the genetic material.
AUGUST **1945**	The United States drops **atom** bombs on Japan.
SEPTEMBER **1945**	Japan surrenders and World War II ends.
1962	Watson, Crick, and Wilkins share the Nobel Prize for their work on DNA.
1968	*The Double **Helix*** by James Watson is published.
1969	U.S. astronauts become the first people to walk on the moon.
1995	Newnham College, Cambridge opens the Rosalind Franklin hall of residence.
1997	Birkbeck College opens the Rosalind Franklin laboratory.
2004	The Chicago Medical School changes its name to the Rosalind Franklin University of Medicine and Science.

GLOSSARY

atom smallest part of any object. Groups of two or more atoms make up a molecule.

cell smallest part of an organism that can function independently. All plants and animals are made up of cells.

chromosome long piece of DNA contained in cells. Each chromosome carries one long DNA molecule.

concentration camp camp where civilians and prisoners of war are taken and imprisoned under extremely harsh conditions.

crystallography type of science that deals with the form and structure of crystals. It is also sometimes called X-ray diffraction.

data new information that needs to be processed or investigated.

dictator ruler who uses force to control a country.

DNA molecule inside plant and animal cells that carries genetic information.

element simple substance that cannot be separated into a simpler substance. Carbon is an example of an element.

feminist someone who believes strongly that women should have equal rights to men.

gene part of the DNA molecule that contains information such as physical traits that are passed from parent to offspring.

genetic characteristics determined by genes that are passed from parent to offspring.

graduate student student who continues studies after he or she has finished university.

graphitizing process of heating coal until it converts to graphite (a form of carbon that conducts electricity). Graphitizing coal turns into graphite, which is used in lead pencils.

helix spiral shape or structure. DNA is in the shape of a double helix.

journal magazine written about a specific subject such as science. Scientists write papers to be published in journals such as *Nature*.

laboratory room used for scientific research and experiments.

makeshift housing structure built to be used for temporary living.

molecule tiny particle made up of groups of atoms. DNA is a molecule.

Nazi member of Adolf Hitler's political party. Nazis controlled Germany from 1933 to 1945.

Nobel Prize international award given every year for outstanding work in science, literature, and world peace.

non-graphitizing coal that is unable to convert to graphite.

Ph.D. highest degree awarded to someone who has done research on a particular subject.

physicist person who studies physics.

physics science of interactions between matter and energy.

radioactivity spontaneous release of energy that can be dangerous to those who are exposed to it. Radioactive substances are used in some medicines and in treatment for cancer.

refugee person who runs away or flees for safety, especially to a different region or country.

RNA shortened form of ribonucleic acid, the genetic material in plants.

scholarship financial gift awarded to a student by an organization. Franklin received a scholarship to work with R. G. W. Norrish.

supervisor person in charge of a student. Franklin was Raymond Gosling's supervisor at King's College.

synagogue place of meeting for worship in the Jewish faith.

virus tiny living thing that is too small to see without a microscope. Viruses cause diseases that can be passed from one person, animal, or plant to another.

X-ray diffraction technique of scattering X-rays through crystals to make a pattern that will reveal the structure of the crystal. It is also sometimes called crystallography.

Want to know more?

Books

DNA & Genetic Engineering, Robert Snedden (Heinemann Library, 2002)
Genes and DNA, Richard Walker (Kingfisher, 2003)
Rosalind Franklin, Cath Senker (Wayland, 2002)

Websites

http://www.ncbe.reading.ac.uk/DNA50/menu.html
The website of the National Centre for Biotechnology Education is very
entertaining as well as informative. Click on "DNA ephemera" to see a lot of
advertising products that use the "Double Helix" design, from door handles to
rubbish bins!

www.pbs.org/wgbh/nova/photo51/
The PBS NOVA science website includes biographical information on
Rosalind Franklin, a study of "Photograph 51", an article defending Franklin's
chance of earning the Nobel Prize had she been alive to receive it, and
detailed information on DNA and RNA.

http://profiles.nlm.nih.gov/KR/Views/Exhibit/narrative/biographical.html
The website of the British National Library of Medicine gives biographical
information and looks into Franklin's work on coal, DNA, and viruses.

www.spartacus.schoolnet.co.uk/SCfranklinR.htm
The Spartacus Educational website gives brief biographical information and
includes passages from some of Franklin's letters to her parents, as well as
observations of Franklin and her work.

Places to visit

National Portrait Gallery
St Martin's Place, London WC2H 0HE
www.npg.org.uk
At the National Portrait Gallery you can see Rosalind Franklin's portrait alongside those of the other scientists credited with discovering DNA.

Science Oxford
1–5 London Place, Oxford OX4 1BD
www.scienceoxford.com
Science Oxford's Hands On Science Gallery has an exhibit on DNA.

Centre for Life
Times Square, Newcastle NE1 4EP
www.life.org.uk
Centre for Life has many exhibitions about human life, including DNA and genes.

INDEX